HOUGHTON MIFFLIN

MATH
Expressions
Common Core

Dr. Karen C. Fuson

GRADE
2

Volume 2

This material is based upon work supported by the
National Science Foundation
under Grant Numbers
ESI-9816320, REC-9806020, and RED-935373.

Any opinions, findings, and conclusions, or recommendations expressed in this material
are those of the author and do not necessarily reflect the views of the National Science Foundation.

HOUGHTON MIFFLIN HARCOURT

Name _____

Homework

Draw coins to show 6 different ways to make
25¢ with pennies, nickels, and dimes.

1. 25¢	**2.** 25¢	**3.** 25¢
4. 25¢	**5.** 25¢	**6.** 25¢

Write how to count the money.

7.

    25¢   50¢   _____   _____   _____   _____

8.

    25¢   50¢   _____   _____   _____

Remembering

1. Write two equations for each Math Mountain.

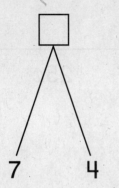

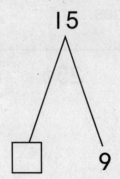

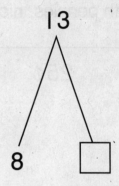

_____   _____   _____

_____   _____   _____

Add.

2. $40 + 60 =$ _____ $50 + 30 =$ _____ $10 + 40 =$ _____

   $4 + 6 =$ _____ $5 + 3 =$ _____ $1 + 4 =$ _____

3. Draw a line segment 6 cm long.
   Mark and count 1-cm lengths to check the length.

4. Stretch Your Thinking Elliot counts a group of coins
   starting with the quarters. His sister counts the same
   coins. She starts counting the pennies. Will they get
   the same amount? Explain.

_____

_____

_____

Explore Quarters

Homework

Under each picture, write the total amount of money so far.
Then write the total using $.

I. 25¢   25¢   10¢   1¢

_____ _____ _____ _____ $ ____.____ ____
                                                    total

2. 100¢   5¢

_____ _____ $ ____.____ ____
                                               total

3. Hope has 1 dollar, 1 quarter, 5 dimes, 3 nickels,

and 2 pennies. Draw 100 s, (25) s, (10) s, (5) s, and (1) s.

Write the total amount of money. $ ____.____ ____
                                                        total

Name _____

Remembering

1. Complete the Math Mountains and equations.

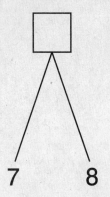

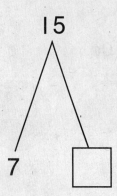

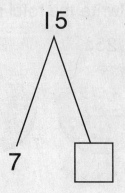

$7 + 8 = \boxed{}$ $7 + \boxed{} = 15$ $15 - 7 = \boxed{}$

Solve. Make a proof drawing.   **Show your work.**

2. Susan wins 78 tickets. She needs 10 tickets
for each prize. How many prizes can she get?
How many tickets will she have left over?

$\boxed{}$ prizes $\boxed{}$ tickets left over

---

3. Write how to count the money.

<u>25¢</u> ____ ____ ____ ____ ____ ____ ____

4. Stretch Your Thinking Maria has $1.35. She
has only quarters and nickels. Draw two possible
groups of coins Maria could have. Use ㉕s to
show quarters and ⑤s to show nickels.

Explore Dollars

Homework

Name

Solve the word problems. Rewrite the 100 or make
a drawing. Add to check your answer.

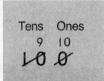

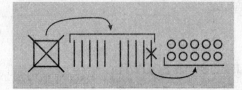

1. There were 100 rubber ducks in the
store. The shopkeeper sold 19 of them.
How many ducks are in the store now?

Show your work.

◻ _____
label

2. Ben bought 100 napkins for the picnic.
There are 26 napkins left after the picnic.
How many napkins were used?

◻ _____
label

Find the unknown addend. Check by adding.

3.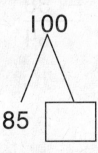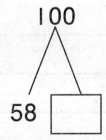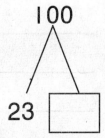

© Houghton Mifflin Harcourt Publishing Company

Name _____

Remembering

Add or subtract.

1.
$\begin{array}{r} 7 \\ +9 \\ \hline \end{array}$
$\begin{array}{r} 8 \\ +5 \\ \hline \end{array}$
$\begin{array}{r} 12 \\ -6 \\ \hline \end{array}$
$\begin{array}{r} 14 \\ -6 \\ \hline \end{array}$
$\begin{array}{r} 7 \\ +4 \\ \hline \end{array}$
$\begin{array}{r} 17 \\ -9 \\ \hline \end{array}$

What number is shown?   H = Hundreds, T = Tens, O = Ones

2.

___ H ___ T ___ O

___ = ___ + ___ + ___

3.

___ H ___ T ___ O

___ = ___ + ___ + ___

Under each picture, write the total amount of money so far. Then write the total using $.

4.   100¢   5¢   1¢

_____   _____   _____

$ ____ . ____ ____
total

5. **Stretch Your Thinking** Ed knows this answer is wrong right away. How could he know this?

$\begin{array}{r} 100 \\ -\ 38 \\ \hline 64 \end{array}$

_____

_____

_____

Addends and Subtraction

Homework

Solve each word problem. Make a
proof drawing if you need to.

Show your work.

1. Amon has 94 tomato seeds. He
uses 27 of them for a science
project. How many seeds does
he have left?

   ☐ _____
           label

2. Benita makes 56 leaf prints. She
gives 29 prints to her cousins. How
many prints does Benita have now?

   ☐ _____
           label

3. Denise has 71 straws. She uses
33 of them to make a bridge. How
many straws does she have left?

   ☐ _____
           label

4. Cedric has 70 sports cards. He gives
away 24 cards to his friends. How
many cards does Cedric have now?

   ☐ _____
           label

Remembering

Estimate and then measure each side.
Then find the distance around the rectangle.

1.

a. Complete the table. Use a
   centimeter ruler to measure.

Side	Estimate	Measure
AB		
BC		
CD		
DA		

b. Find the distance around the rectangle.

_____ cm + _____ cm + _____ cm + _____ cm = _____ cm

Solve the word problem. Rewrite the 100 or
make a drawing. Add to check your answer.   **Show your work.**

2. Amy has a box with 100 craft sticks in it. She
   uses some of them to make a project. There
   are 64 craft sticks left in the box. How many
   craft sticks did she use?

   ☐ _____
              label

3. **Stretch Your Thinking** Write a subtraction word
   problem with 29 as the answer.

   _____

   _____

   _____

Subtraction Word Problems

Name _____

Homework

Expanded Method	Ungroup First Method	Proof Drawing

Expanded Method

$$93 = \cancel{90} + \cancel{3} \quad {}^{80} + {}^{13}$$
$$- 57 = 50 + 7$$
$$\overline{} \quad \overline{30 + 6 = 36}$$

Ungroup First Method

$$\cancel{9}\cancel{3} \quad {}^{8}{}^{13}$$
$$- 5 7$$
$$\overline{3 6}$$

Proof Drawing

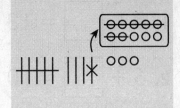

Subtract using any method.

1. $\begin{array}{r} 38 \\ -21 \\ \hline \end{array}$

2. $\begin{array}{r} 57 \\ -39 \\ \hline \end{array}$

3. $\begin{array}{r} 95 \\ -64 \\ \hline \end{array}$

4. $\begin{array}{r} 50 \\ -13 \\ \hline \end{array}$

5. $\begin{array}{r} 68 \\ -15 \\ \hline \end{array}$

6. $\begin{array}{r} 77 \\ -29 \\ \hline \end{array}$

7. $\begin{array}{r} 74 \\ -48 \\ \hline \end{array}$

8. $\begin{array}{r} 84 \\ -49 \\ \hline \end{array}$

Remembering

Write the unknown addend (partner).

1. $5 + \boxed{} = 13$ $15 - 9 = \boxed{}$ $4 + \boxed{} = 11$

2. $6 + \boxed{} = 10$ $13 - 6 = \boxed{}$ $12 - 7 = \boxed{}$

3. Under the coins, write the total amount of money so far.
   Then write the total using $.

____ ____ ____ ____ ____ ____ $ ____ . ____
                                      total   total

Solve the word problem. Make a proof drawing
if you need to.

Show your work.

4. Jackson has 62 pennies in his jar. He
   spends 38 of them. How many pennies
   does he have now?

$\boxed{}$ _____
                label

5. **Stretch Your Thinking** How do you know if you need
   to ungroup a ten for ones when subtracting?

_____

_____

_____

_____

Two Methods of Subtraction

Homework

Subtract.

1. 87
   −59
   ____

2. 63
   −14
   ____

3. 55
   −18
   ____

4. 73
   −17
   ____

5. 83
   −12
   ____

6. 99
   −35
   ____

7. 62
   −55
   ____

8. 71
   −49
   ____

9. 45
   −26
   ____

10. 50
    −11
    ____

11. 92
    −44
    ____

12. 75
    −52
    ____

Practice and Explain a Method **101**

Name _____

Remembering

Make a drawing. Write an equation.
Solve the problem.

Show your work.

1. Lily has 14 markers. Her
   sister took some. Now Lily
   has 8 markers. How many
   did Lily's sister take?

   ☐☐☐ _____

   label

Add.

2.　　57　　　　　　　73　　　　　　　89
　　+ 35　　　　　　+ 48　　　　　　+ 61

Subtract using any method.

3.　　64　　　　　　　95　　　　　　　70
　　− 27　　　　　　− 37　　　　　　− 41

4. **Stretch Your Thinking** Write and
   solve a subtraction exercise where
   you do not ungroup. Write and solve
   a subtraction exercise where you
   must ungroup.

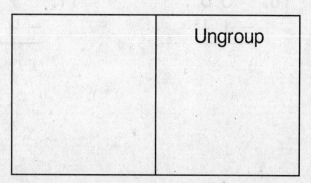

Ungroup

　　　　　　　　Practice and Explain a Method

Homework

Solve each word problem. Draw a
proof drawing if you need to.

Show your work.

---

1. There are 200 water bottles on a
   table. The runners in a race take
   73 of them. How many water bottles
   are left on the table?

   _____
                label

---

2. There are 200 weeds in Kelly's
   garden. Her little sister pulls out
   44 of them. How many weeds are
   still in the garden?

   _____
                label

Subtract.

3.
```
  2 0 0
-   6 6
```

4.
```
  2 0 0
-   8 2
```

5.
```
  2 0 0
-   5 4
```

6.
```
  2 0 0
-   9 5
```

7.
```
  2 0 0
-   3 8
```

8.
```
  2 0 0
-   4 7
```

Remembering

Make a drawing. Write an equation.
Solve the problem.

Show your work.

1. Sean finds 5 orange leaves and some
yellow leaves. He finds 14 leaves in all.
How many yellow leaves does he find?

☐ _____
label

Add. Use any method.

2.   48   64   74
   + 75   + 46   + 89

Subtract.

3.   56   82   61
   − 19   − 53   − 46

4. **Stretch Your Thinking** Suppose you subtract
a 2-digit number from 200. Will you have to ungroup
hundreds or tens? Explain. Give an example.

_____

_____

_____

_____

Homework

Decide if you need to ungroup. Then subtract.

1. $\begin{array}{r} 147 \\ -\ 32 \\ \hline \end{array}$

2. $\begin{array}{r} 147 \\ -\ 38 \\ \hline \end{array}$

3. $\begin{array}{r} 147 \\ -\ 48 \\ \hline \end{array}$

4. $\begin{array}{r} 126 \\ -\ 54 \\ \hline \end{array}$

5. $\begin{array}{r} 126 \\ -\ 57 \\ \hline \end{array}$

6. $\begin{array}{r} 126 \\ -\ 97 \\ \hline \end{array}$

7. $\begin{array}{r} 187 \\ -\ 46 \\ \hline \end{array}$

8. $\begin{array}{r} 187 \\ -\ 49 \\ \hline \end{array}$

9. $\begin{array}{r} 187 \\ -\ 99 \\ \hline \end{array}$

10. $\begin{array}{r} 172 \\ -\ 35 \\ \hline \end{array}$

11. $\begin{array}{r} 172 \\ -\ 85 \\ \hline \end{array}$

12. $\begin{array}{r} 172 \\ -\ 31 \\ \hline \end{array}$

Name _____

Remembering

Make a drawing. Write an equation. **Show your work.**
Solve the problem.

1. The coach gives out 8 large water
   bottles and 8 small water bottles.
   How many water bottles does the
   coach give out?

   ☐ _____
              label

Add. Use any method.

2. 66   97   53
   + 77   + 84   + 79
   ————   ————   ————

Subtract.

3. 2 0 0   2 0 0   2 0 0
    − 4 1   − 7 3   − 5 7
    ————————   ————————   ————————

4. **Stretch Your Thinking** Use the numbers
   below to complete the subtraction problem.
   Place the numbers so that you must ungroup
   two times. Then subtract.

   3   6   9   5

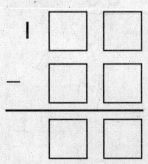

Ungroup from the Left or from the Right

Name _____

Homework

Decide if you need to ungroup. Then subtract.

1. $\begin{array}{r} 130 \\ -99 \\ \hline \end{array}$
2. $\begin{array}{r} 150 \\ -39 \\ \hline \end{array}$
3. $\begin{array}{r} 160 \\ -67 \\ \hline \end{array}$

4. $\begin{array}{r} 108 \\ -88 \\ \hline \end{array}$
5. $\begin{array}{r} 120 \\ -83 \\ \hline \end{array}$
6. $\begin{array}{r} 101 \\ -72 \\ \hline \end{array}$

Solve each word problem.   **Show your work.**

7. There were 120 nickels in a jar.
   Janice took out 49 nickels. How
   many nickels are in the jar now?

   ☐ _____
        label

8. Last week, there were 109 books
   at the bookstore. So far, 25 books
   have been sold. How many
   books have not been sold?

   ☐ _____
        label

     Zero in the Ones or Tens Place **107**

Name _____

Remembering

Add. Use doubles.

1. $6 + 7 =$ ☐ $8 + 7 =$ ☐ $6 + 5 =$ ☐

2. $9 + 7 =$ ☐ $11 + 9 =$ ☐ $8 + 6 =$ ☐

Estimate and then measure each side.
Then find the distance around the triangle.

3.

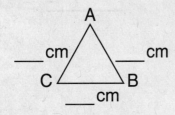

a. Complete the table.

Side	Estimate	Measure
AB		
BC		
CA		

b. Find the distance around the triangle.

_____ cm + _____ cm + _____ cm = _____ cm

Decide if you need to ungroup. Then subtract.

4.
```
  1 6 9
-   4 4
```

```
  1 8 5
-   7 9
```

```
  1 3 2
-   6 8
```

5. **Stretch Your Thinking** Look at Evan's
subtraction problem. What did he do wrong?
Find the correct answer.

```
  1 0 7
-   6 8
-------
    4 9
```

_____

_____

Zero in the Ones or Tens Place

Homework

What would you like to buy? First, see how
much money you have. Pay for the item.
How much money do you have left?

Yard Sale

Globe	Ring	Sports Bag	Eraser	Color Pencils
85¢	67¢	98¢	79¢	66¢

1. I have 124¢ in my pocket.

I bought the _____ .

```
  1 2 4¢
−       ¢
_____
```

I have _____ ¢ left.

2. I have 152¢ in my pocket.

I bought the _____ .

```
  1 5 2¢
−       ¢
_____
```

I have _____ ¢ left.

3. I have 145¢ in my pocket.

I bought the _____ .

```
  1 4 5¢
−       ¢
_____
```

I have _____ ¢ left.

4. I have 131¢ in my pocket.

I bought the _____ .

```
  1 3 1¢
−       ¢
_____
```

I have _____ ¢ left.

Model Subtraction with Money **109**

Remembering

Find the total or partner.

1.   7   9   8   15   12   16
    + 6   + 5   + 9   − 6   − 8   − 9
   ____   ____   ____   ____   ____   ____

Label the shapes using the words in the box.

| cube | quadrilateral | pentagon | hexagon |

2.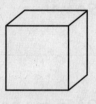

_____

3.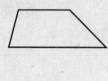

_____

Solve the word problem.   **Show your work.**

4. Logan buys a notebook with
   106 pages. He uses 29 of the
   pages. How many pages are
   not used?

   ☐ _____
        label

5. **Stretch Your Thinking** Kayla has 135¢. She buys
   a toy and has 78¢ left. What is the price of the toy
   she buys?

   _____

Model Subtraction with Money

Homework

Subtract.

1. 29
  − 13

2. 54
  − 26

3. 75
  − 25

4. 48
  − 38

5. 90
  − 57

6. 17
  − 8

7. 100
  − 42

8. 63
  − 22

9. 97
  − 59

10. Explain how you found the difference for Exercise 7.

_____

_____

_____

Name _____

Remembering

Make a matching drawing or draw comparison
bars. Solve the problem.   **Show your work.**

1. Jayden has 8 grapes. Ashley has
   6 more grapes than Jayden has.
   How many grapes does Ashley
   have?

   ┌─────────┐
   │   │ _____
   └─────────┘
        label

Which sticker would you like to buy? First, see how
much money you have. Pay for the sticker. How
much money do you have left?

Sticker Sale

Smile	Heart	Sun	Moon
78¢	89¢	76¢	97¢

2. I have 132¢ in my pocket.

   I bought the _____.

   $$132¢$$
   $$- \quad ¢$$
   _____

   I have _____ ¢ left.

3. I have 164¢ in my pocket.

   I bought the _____.

   $$164¢$$
   $$- \quad ¢$$
   _____

   I have _____ ¢ left.

4. **Stretch Your Thinking** Subtract.
   Which subtraction takes longer to do? Explain.

   A $\begin{array}{r} 64 \\ -\ 31 \\ \hline \end{array}$ **B** $\begin{array}{r} 92 \\ -\ 47 \\ \hline \end{array}$

   _____

Fluency: Subtraction within 100

Homework

Draw a Math Mountain to solve each word problem. Show how you add or subtract.

Show your work.

1. Papi has 148 slices of pizza in his shop. He sells 56 slices. How many slices does Papi have left?

☐ _____
label

2. There are 34 children at the park. Then 16 children join them. How many children are at the park now?

☐ _____
label

3. Bella has 19 crayons. She gives 12 of them to her friend. How many crayons does she have left?

☐ _____
label

4. Seventy-nine girls and forty-eight boys are in Grade 2 at Center School. How many children are in Grade 2?

☐ _____
label

Remembering

Make a drawing. Write an equation.
Solve the problem.

Show your work.

1. Luke has 7 trucks. Zoe has 6 more
trucks than Luke. How many trucks
does Zoe have?

☐   _____
         label

2. Show the data from the table on the line plot.

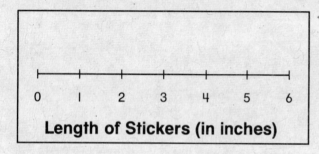

Length of Stickers (in inches)
5 inches
3 inches
4 inches
2 inches
3 inches

Subtract.

3.   54
    − 31

4.   81
    − 26

5.   74
    − 7

6. **Stretch Your Thinking** Write and solve
a subtraction word problem that starts with
146. The answer should be less than 100.

_____

_____

     Word Problems with Addition and Subtraction

Name _____

Homework

1. Write all of the equations for 74, 25, and 49.

$25 + 49 = 74$ _____ $74 = 25 + 49$ _____

_____   _____

_____   _____

_____   _____

2. Write all of the equations for 157, 68, and 89.

$68 + 89 = 157$ _____ $157 = 68 + 89$ _____

_____   _____

_____   _____

_____   _____

Remembering

Add in any order. Write the total.

1. $6 + 3 + 5 = \boxed{}$ $9 + 2 + 9 = \boxed{}$ $3 + 5 + 7 = \boxed{}$

2. $8 + 7 + 2 = \boxed{}$ $7 + 3 + 8 = \boxed{}$ $5 + 8 + 4 = \boxed{}$

Make a drawing for each number. Write $<$, $>$, or $=$.

3. 122 $\bigcirc$ 131

4. 35 $\bigcirc$ 28

Draw a Math Mountain to solve the word problem. Show how you add or subtract.

Show your work.

5. Berry Elementary School has 127 children. 69 of the children are girls. How many children are boys?

$\boxed{}$ _____
         label

6. **Stretch Your Thinking** When would there be only four different equations for a set of Math Mountain numbers? Give an example.

_____

Equations with Greater Numbers

Homework

Add or subtract. Watch the sign!

1. $\begin{array}{r} 75 \\ +25 \\ \hline \end{array}$

2. $\begin{array}{r} 14 \\ +6 \\ \hline \end{array}$

3. $\begin{array}{r} 47 \\ +38 \\ \hline \end{array}$

4. $\begin{array}{r} 87 \\ -48 \\ \hline \end{array}$

5. $\begin{array}{r} 34 \\ +18 \\ \hline \end{array}$

6. $\begin{array}{r} 27 \\ -8 \\ \hline \end{array}$

7. $\begin{array}{r} 100 \\ -85 \\ \hline \end{array}$

8. $\begin{array}{r} 67 \\ -29 \\ \hline \end{array}$

9. $\begin{array}{r} 58 \\ +37 \\ \hline \end{array}$

10. $\begin{array}{r} 81 \\ -53 \\ \hline \end{array}$

11. $\begin{array}{r} 47 \\ +37 \\ \hline \end{array}$

12. $\begin{array}{r} 99 \\ -39 \\ \hline \end{array}$

Remembering

Make a drawing. Write an equation.
Solve the problem.

Show your work.

1. Mayumi shops with her mom.
   She puts 8 oranges in the basket.
   Her mom puts in 7 more oranges.
   How many oranges are in the
   basket now?

   □ _____
   　　　　label

---

2. Write all of the equations for 83, 35, 48.

　　83
　35　48

$35 + 48 = 83$　　　　　$83 = 35 + 48$

_____　　　　_____

_____　　　　_____

_____　　　　_____

3. **Stretch Your Thinking** Allison solved this
   problem. Is she correct? If not, explain and solve.

   $$\begin{array}{r} 46 \\ +\,17 \\ \hline 53 \end{array}$$

   _____

   _____

Practice Addition and Subtraction

Mr. Green wants to buy some things at a
flea market. He will pay for the items with
one dollar (100 cents). How much change
will he get back?

Mittens	Toy Binoculars	Toy Camera	Toy Lamb	Plant
17¢	39¢	46¢	28¢	52¢

1. Mr. Green buys the mittens
and the plant.

_____ ¢

+ _____ ¢

Total: _____

100¢ − _____ = _____

His change will be _____ ¢.

2. Mr. Green buys the toy lamb
and the toy camera.

_____ ¢

+ _____ ¢

Total: _____

100¢ − _____ = _____

His change will be _____ ¢.

3. Mr. Green buys the toy
binoculars and the toy lamb.

_____ ¢

+ _____ ¢

Total: _____

100¢ − _____ = _____

His change will be _____ ¢.

4. Mr. Green buys the toy camera
and the plant.

_____ ¢

+ _____ ¢

Total: _____

100¢ − _____ = _____

His change will be _____ ¢.

Remembering

Add or subtract.

1.

5	9	6	13	18	14
+4	+6	+8	−8	−9	−9

Cross out the extra information or write hidden or
missing information. Then solve the problem.

Show your work.

2. Latisha has some apples. She buys
   5 more. How many apples does
   she have now?

   _____

   [ ] _____
   label

Add or subtract. Watch the sign!

3.

73	56	100
−38	+27	−47

4. **Stretch Your Thinking** Rashid has one dollar
   (100 cents). He wants to buy a ball for 50 cents.
   He also wants to buy two other toys and still have
   money left over. Explain what Rashid needs to
   do when choosing the two toys.

   _____

   _____

   _____

Name _____

Homework

Add up to solve each word problem.   **Show your work.**

---

1. Rudy has 45 ants in his ant farm. He adds some
   more ants to the ant farm. Now there are 69 ants.
   How many ants does Rudy add to the ant farm?

   [ ] _____
              label

---

2. Tina has 92 flowers in her garden this morning.
   After she takes some flowers to school, there
   are 33 flowers in her garden. How many flowers
   does Tina take to school?

   [ ] _____
              label

---

3. Lia collects 86 buttons. Then she gives some
   to Matt. Now Lia has 61 buttons. How many
   buttons does Lia give to Matt?

   [ ] _____
              label

---

4. There were 73 cars in the garage this morning.
   Now there are 24 cars in the garage. How
   many cars left the garage?

   [ ] _____
              label

Remembering

Add. Use doubles.

1. 5 + 6 = ☐   9 + 7 = ☐   10 + 8 = ☐

2. 7 + 8 = ☐   8 + 8 = ☐   7 + 6 = ☐

Mia and Tom buy things at the school store. They will
each pay for the items with one dollar (100 cents).
How much change will they each get back?

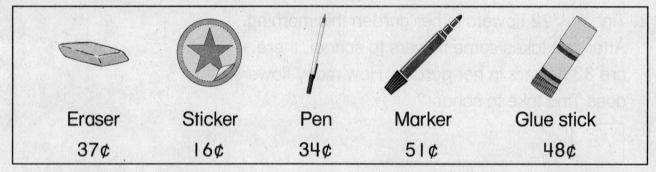

Eraser	Sticker	Pen	Marker	Glue stick
37¢	16¢	34¢	51¢	48¢

3. Mia buys the marker and the
sticker.

_____ ¢

+ _____ ¢

Total: _____ ¢

100¢ − _____ = _____

Her change will be _____ ¢.

4. Tom buys the eraser and the
glue stick.

_____ ¢

+ _____ ¢

Total: _____ ¢

100¢ − _____ = _____

His change will be _____ ¢.

---

5. Stretch Your Thinking Use the pictures and prices above.
Suppose Mia has another 100 cents and buys one item. If she
has 66¢ left, how can you tell which item she bought? Explain.

_____

_____

Word Problems with Unknown Addends

Solve each word problem.   **Show your work.**

1. Alma and Larry have stickers to put on their poster. Alma has 28 stickers. They have 84 stickers in all. How many stickers does Larry have?

☐ _____
label

2. There are 61 magazines in the library. Then more magazines are delivered. Now there are 100 magazines. How many new magazines are delivered to the library?

☐ _____
label

3. Mori puts 95 pretzels in a bowl. Her friends eat some. Now there are 72 pretzels in the bowl. How many pretzels do her friends eat?

☐ _____
label

4. Eric's basketball team scores 36 points in the first game. They score some points in the second game. In the two games, they score 52 points in all. How many points do they score in the second game?

☐ _____
label

Name _____

Remembering

Use your centimeter ruler. Measure the horizontal line
segment below by marking and counting 1-cm lengths.

1.

_____ □ cm

Add ones or tens.

2. $5 + 6 =$ □ $8 + 7 =$ □ $9 + 4 =$ □

   $50 + 60 =$ □ $80 + 70 =$ □ $90 + 40 =$ □

Add up to solve the word problem.   **Show your work.**

3. Austin has 65 United States stamps. He
   gets more stamps from other countries.
   Now he has 84 stamps. How many stamps
   are from other countries?

   □ _____
           label

4. **Stretch Your Thinking** Look at Problem 3. Did you
   add to solve the problem? Explain.

   _____

   _____

   _____

More Word Problems with Unknown Addends

Homework

Make a drawing. Write an equation. Solve.

1. Mariko has 63 photos in her photo book.
   That is 23 fewer photos than Sharon has.
   How many photos does Sharon have?

   ☐ _____
      label

2. Fred has some crayons. He gives Drew
   26 crayons. Now Fred has 42 crayons.
   How many crayons did Fred start with?

   ☐ _____
      label

3. Marisa brings out 60 bowls for the party.
   Thirty-five of the bowls are large. The
   rest are small. How many small bowls
   does Marisa bring out?

   ☐ _____
      label

4. Sean sells 35 tickets for the school play.
   If he sells 24 more tickets, he will sell all
   the tickets he had at the start. How many
   tickets did Sean start with?

   ☐ _____
      label

Remembering

Add.

1. $15 + 29 + 34 =$ _____

2. $23 + 38 + 27 + 59 =$ _____

Solve the word problem.   **Show your work.**

3. Carter has 5 jersey shirts, 4 solid
   shirts, and some plaid shirts. He
   has 15 shirts altogether. How
   many plaid shirts does he have?

   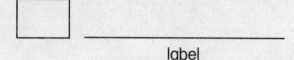
   label

Draw comparison bars and write an equation to
solve the problem.

4. Max has 72 pennies. Jada has
   34 fewer pennies than Max. How
   many pennies does Jada have?

   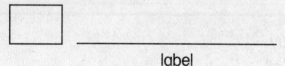
   label

5. **Stretch Your Thinking** Write and solve a
   word problem that matches the drawing.

   _____

   _____

   _____

Ryan	55	
Erin	?	29

Mixed Word Problems

Homework

Think about the first-step question.
Then solve the problem.

I. Luisa has 35 building blocks. Jack gives
her 18 more blocks. Luisa uses 26 blocks
to build a castle. How many blocks are
not used in the castle?

[ ] _____

label

---

2. There are 45 red apples and 24 green
apples for sale at a farm stand. The farmer
sells some apples. Now she has 36 apples
left. How many apples does the farmer sell?

[ ] _____

label

---

3. Maria has 16 more beads than Gus.
Gus has 24 beads. Denise has 12 more
beads than Maria. How many beads does
Denise have?

[ ] _____

label

Remembering

Find the total or partner.

1.
$$7 \atop +8$$
$$6 \atop +8$$
$$9 \atop +6$$
$$16 \atop -8$$
$$12 \atop -7$$
$$17 \atop -9$$

2. Look for shapes in your classroom and school.
   List or draw objects that show triangles.

Make a drawing. Write an equation. Solve.

3. Eric has 53 baseball cards.
   17 cards are new. The rest are old.
   How many baseball cards
   are old?

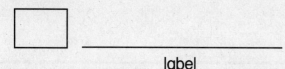

                           label

4. **Stretch Your Thinking** Write a 2-step
   word problem that uses subtraction then
   addition. Solve.

   _____

   _____

2-Step Word Problems

© Houghton Mifflin Harcourt Publishing Company

Homework

Think about the first-step question.
Then solve the problem.

___

1. There are 45 children at the park in the morning.
   25 are boys and the rest are girls. Some more
   girls come to the park in the afternoon. Now there
   are 30 girls at the park. How many girls come
   to the park in the afternoon?

   ☐ _____
              label

___

2. Jonah has 36 sheets of green paper and
   26 sheets of blue paper. He gives some
   sheets of green paper to Tova. Now he has
   42 sheets of paper. How many sheets of
   green paper does he give Tova?

   ☐ _____
              label

___

3. There are 16 mystery books, 22 history books,
   and 21 science books in a large bookcase.
   A smaller bookcase has 30 fewer books.
   How many books are in the smaller bookcase?

   ☐ _____
              label

Remembering

Estimate and then measure each side.
Then find the distance around the rectangle.

1.

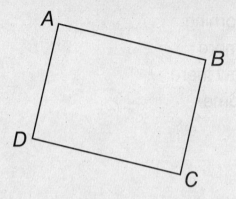

a. Complete the table. Use a centimeter ruler to measure.

Side	Estimate	Measure
AB		
BC		
CD		
DA		

b. Find the distance around the rectangle.

_____ cm + _____ cm + _____ cm + _____ cm = _____ cm

Think about the first-step question. Then solve the problem.

2. Kate has 37 old crayons and 45 new crayons. She gives some crayons to Sam. Now she has 56 crayons. How many crayons did she give to Sam?

☐ _____
            label

3. **Stretch Your Thinking** Use the information in the table to write a 2-step word problem. Then solve.

_____

_____

Points Scored	
Will	47
Ava	29
Cody	35

Homework

The children on the math team each measured the length of one of their feet. They made a table to show their data.

Length of Foot

Name	Length
Marta	19 cm
Pete	18 cm
Alberto	20 cm
Miko	13 cm
Sasha	16 cm

Use the table to solve each word problem.   **Show your work.**

1. How much longer is Alberto's foot than Pete's?

   ☐ _____
       label

2. Which child has a foot that is 3 cm longer than Sasha's?

   _____

3. Miko's foot is 2 cm shorter than Jon's. What is the length of Jon's foot?

   ☐ _____
       label

4. Use the information in the table to write your own problem. Solve the problem.

   _____

   _____

   _____

Remembering

Complete the addition doubles equation.

1. ☐ + ☐ = 14

2. ☐ + ☐ = 8

3. ☐ + ☐ = 6

4. ☐ + ☐ = 18

Add.

5.   46   34   69
   + 28   + 57   + 52

Think about the first-step question. Then
solve the problem.

6. The coach gets a delivery of 24 large uniforms,
18 medium uniforms, and 25 small uniforms.
He returns 19 of the uniforms. How many
uniforms does the coach have now?

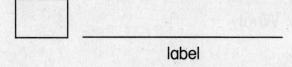

           label

7. **Stretch Your Thinking** Use a centimeter
ruler to measure four objects. Record each
length. Then write a question and solve.

Object	Length

_____

_____

_____

Homework

Write the time in two different ways.

1.

_____ o'clock

2.

_____ o'clock

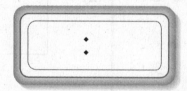

3.

_____ o'clock

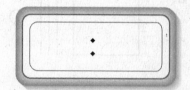

Draw the hands on each analog clock and write the time on each digital clock below.

4.

1 o'clock

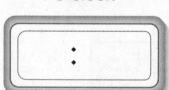

5.

6 o'clock

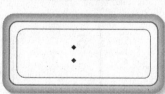

6.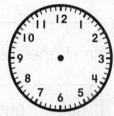

12 o'clock

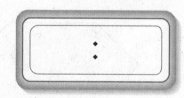

For each activity, ring the appropriate time.

7. eat an afternoon snack

    3:00 A.M.   2:00 P.M.   6:00 P.M.

8. go to a movie after dinner

    8:00 A.M.   12:00 NOON   7:00 P.M.

Remembering

Add.

1.
```
   4        6        3        5        8        9
 + 7      + 9      + 7      + 2      + 8      + 1
```

What number is shown?   H = Hundreds, T = Tens, O = Ones

```
┌────────────────────────────────┬────────────────────────────────┐
│ 2.   ┌─────┐  ‖‖  ○ ○ ○ ○ ○    │ 3.   ┌─────┐  ‖‖‖  ○ ○         │
│      │     │         ○          │      │     │                   │
│      │     │                    │      │     │                   │
│      └─────┘                    │      └─────┘                   │
│                                 │                                 │
│      ____ H ____ T ____ O       │      ____ H ____ T ____ O       │
│   ____ = ____ + ____ + ____     │   ____ = ____ + ____ + ____     │
└────────────────────────────────┴────────────────────────────────┘
```

Label the shapes using the words in the box.

```
┌──────────────────────────────────────────────────┐
│   cube    quadrilateral    pentagon    hexagon     │
└──────────────────────────────────────────────────┘
```

4.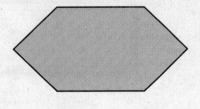

_____

5.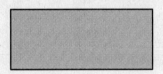

_____

6. **Stretch Your Thinking** Name the same activity you
   might do at 9:00 A.M. and at 9:00 P.M.

   _____

Hours and A.M. or P.M.

Name _____

Homework

Write the time on the digital clocks.

1.

2.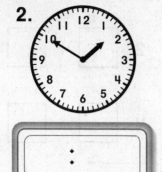

3.

4.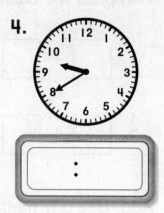

:

:

:

:

Draw hands on each clock to show the time.

5.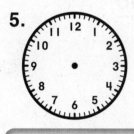

6.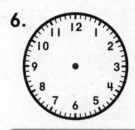

7.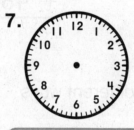

8.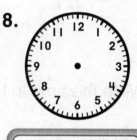

8:15

11:20

12:30

1:45

For each activity, ring the appropriate time.

9. trip to the zoo

    11:10 A.M.

    11:10 P.M.

10. building sand castles

    10:00 A.M.

    10:00 P.M.

11. bedtime story

    8:15 A.M.

    8:15 P.M.

12. shadow puppets

    9:30 A.M.

    9:30 P.M.

Remembering

Complete the addition doubles equation.

1. ☐ + ☐ = 8

2. ☐ + ☐ = 18

3. ☐ + ☐ = 12

4. ☐ + ☐ = 16

Add. Use any method.

5.
```
   53
+ 89
```

6.
```
   72
+ 48
```

7.
```
   95
+ 66
```

Write the time in two different ways.

8.

_____ o'clock

9.

_____ o'clock

10.

_____ o'clock

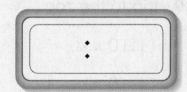

11. **Stretch Your Thinking** Name three different
times when both hands are between the 12 and
the 3 on the clock.

_____

Hours and Minutes

Homework

Use the picture graph to answer the questions.

Book Sales

Peter	📕	📕	📕	📕	📕					
Tammy	📕	📕	📕	📕						
Shana	📕	📕	📕	📕	📕	📕	📕	📕	📕	

1. Who sold the most books? _____

2. Who sold the fewest books? _____

3. How many more books did Shana sell than Tammy?

   ☐ _____

   label

4. How many fewer books did Peter sell than Shana?

   ☐ _____

   label

5. How many more books did Peter sell than Tammy?

   ☐ _____

   label

6. How many books did the children sell altogether?

   ☐ _____

   label

7. **Write Your Own** Write and solve your own question about the graph.

_____

_____

Discuss Picture Graphs **141**

Remembering

Add ones or tens.

1. $5 + 9 =$ ☐ $4 + 7 =$ ☐ $6 + 7 =$ ☐

    $50 + 90 =$ ☐ $40 + 70 =$ ☐ $60 + 70 =$ ☐

Solve the word problem. Rewrite the 100 or make
a drawing. Add to check your work.

2. Savanna had 100 pennies in a jar. She spent some
   of them. She has 27 in the jar now. How many
   pennies did she spend?

   ☐ _____
        label

Draw hands on each clock to show the time.

3.

4.

5.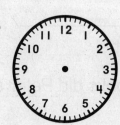

6.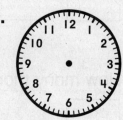

5:10   2:50   10:25   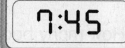7:45

7. **Stretch Your Thinking** Without counting, how can
   you tell which item has the most on a picture graph?

   _____

   _____

Discuss Picture Graphs

Homework

Name _____

Read the picture graph.
Write the number. Ring *more* or *fewer*.

Number of Goldfish

Mina	🐟 🐟 🐟 🐟
Emily	🐟 🐟 🐟 🐟 🐟 🐟 🐟
Raj	🐟 🐟 🐟 🐟 🐟

1. Mina has ☐ *more fewer* goldfish than Emily.

2. Raj needs ☐ *more fewer* fish to have as many as Emily has.

Solve.

Number of Bells

Dan	🔔 🔔 🔔 🔔 🔔 🔔 🔔 🔔
Tani	🔔 🔔 🔔
Loren	🔔 🔔 🔔 🔔 🔔 🔔

3. How many bells do the children have altogether?

☐ _____
  label

4. Dan has 6 red bells. The rest are yellow. How many of Dan's bells are yellow?

☐ _____
  label

Remembering

Add in any order. Write the total.

1. $1 + 5 + 9 =$ ☐   2. $6 + 6 + 5 =$ ☐

3. $2 + 4 + 3 + 3 =$ ☐   4. $3 + 8 + 5 + 7 =$ ☐

Use the picture graph to answer the questions.

Pens

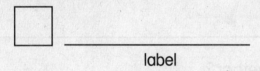

| Sophia | ✏ | ✏ | ✏ | ✏ | ✏ | ✏ | ✏ | ✏ | | |
| David | ✏ | ✏ | ✏ | ✏ | ✏ | | | | | |

Jeremy

5. Who has the most pens? _____

6. Who has the fewest pens? _____

7. How many more pens does Sophia have
   than David?

   ☐ _____

   label

8. **Stretch Your Thinking** Without counting all of the
   pens, explain how you can find how many fewer pens
   Jeremy has than David.

   _____

   _____

   _____

Read Picture Graphs

Name _____

Homework

1. The park has 9 oak trees, 2 maple trees, and 6 elm trees in it. Complete the data table.

Trees in the Park

Oak	
Maple	
Elm	

2. Use the data table to complete the bar graph.

Trees in the Park

Oak											
Maple											
Elm											

0   1   2   3   4   5   6   7   8   9   10

Use your bar graph. Write the number and ring *more* or *fewer*.

3. There are ☐ *more fewer* oak trees than maple trees in the park.

4. There are ☐ *more fewer* maple trees than elm trees in the park.

5. We need to plant ☐ *more fewer* elm trees to have as many elm trees as oak trees.

Remembering

Add.

1. 20 + 40 = _____   10 + 90 = _____   50 + 30 = _____

   2 + 4 = _____   1 + 9 = _____   5 + 3 = _____

Read the picture graph.
Write the number. Ring *more* or *fewer.*

Number of Crayons

Ellen	✏ ✏ ✏ ✏
Brad	✏ ✏ ✏ ✏ ✏ ✏ ✏
Yoko	✏ ✏ ✏ ✏ ✏ ✏ ✏ ✏ ✏

2. Brad has ☐ *more fewer* crayons than Yoko.

3. Ellen needs ☐ *more fewer* crayons to have

   as many crayons as Brad.

4. Five of Yoko's crayons are new. The rest of
   her crayons are old. How many are old?

   ☐ _____
        label

5. **Stretch Your Thinking** Explain how a bar graph
   and a picture graph are alike.

   _____

   _____

   _____

Homework

Nineteen children each play a musical instrument.

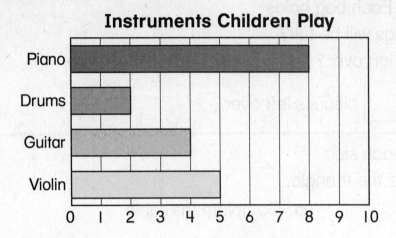

Instruments Children Play

Use the bar graph to complete the sentences.

1. Two fewer children play the _____ than the guitar.

2. Nine children play the _____

   or the _____.

3. [ ] more children have to play the guitar to have

   the same number as the children who play the piano.

4. [ ] fewer children play the violin than play the piano.

5. [ ] children play the piano or the drums.

6. [ ] children play the piano, the guitar, or the violin.

Remembering

Solve. Make a proof drawing.   **Show your work.**

1. Megan bakes 57 biscuits. Each bag holds
   10 biscuits. How many bags will be full?
   How many biscuits will be left over?

   ☐ bags   ☐ biscuits left over

Estimate and then measure each side.
Then find the distance around the triangle.

2.

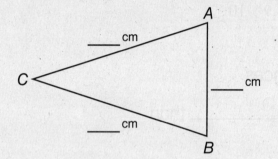

a. Complete the table.

Side	Estimate	Measure
AB		
BC		
CA		

b. Find the distance around the triangle.

_____ cm + _____ cm + _____ cm = _____ cm

---

3. Nathan has 6 cars, 4 trucks, and
   8 buses in his toy garage.
   Complete the table to show this.

Nathan's Garage

Cars	
Trucks	
Buses	

4. **Stretch Your Thinking** Look at the completed table
   in Exercise 3. Explain how the bars would look if the
   information were in a bar graph.

   _____

   _____

   _____

Read Bar Graphs

Homework

Use the bar graph to answer the questions below.
Fill in the circle next to the correct answer.

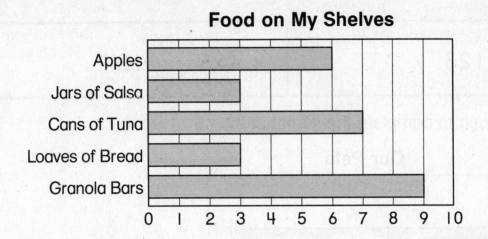

Food on My Shelves

1. How many more cans of tuna are there than jars of salsa?

   ○ 4
   ○ 5
   ○ 6
   ○ 7

2. Altogether, how many apples and granola bars do I have?

   ○ 11
   ○ 13
   ○ 15
   ○ 16

3. I eat some apples. Now there are only 4 apples left. How many apples did I eat?

   ○ 0
   ○ 1
   ○ 2
   ○ 4

4. **Write Your Own** Write 1 question about the graph. Answer your question.

_____

_____

Remembering

Write <, >, or =.

1. 164 ◯ 146

2. 79 ◯ 79

3. 88 ◯ 123

4. 125 ◯ 124

Use the bar graph to complete the sentences.

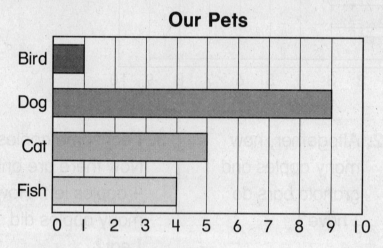

Our Pets

5. Three fewer children have _____ than fish.

6. Thirteen children have _____ or _____.

7. _____ more children need to have cats to have the same number as the children who have dogs.

8. Stretch Your Thinking Look at the bar graph. Name three ways that the information could change so that there would be the same number of birds and cats.

_____

_____

Solve Problems Using a Bar Graphs

Homework

1. Prince won 8 medals at the dog show.
   Lady won 5 medals. Muffy won 3 medals.
   Make a table to show this.

_____

Dog	Medals

2. Use the information in the table to make a
   picture graph. Use a circle for each 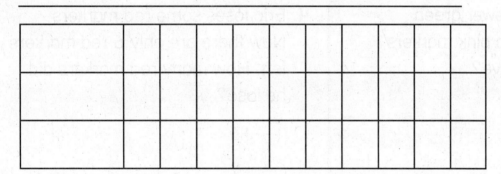 .

3. Use the information in the table to make a bar graph.

_____

_____									
_____									
_____									

     Name _____

Remembering

Subtract using any method.

1. $\begin{array}{r} 73 \\ -\ 42 \\ \hline \end{array}$ 2. $\begin{array}{r} 60 \\ -\ 18 \\ \hline \end{array}$

Use the bar graph to answer the questions below.
Fill in the circle next to the correct answer.

Eric's Markers

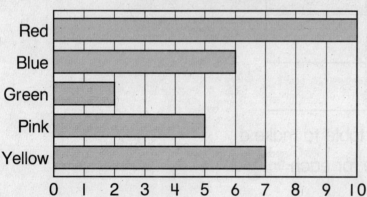

3. How many fewer green markers than pink markers does Eric have?

○ 5
○ 4
○ 3
○ 2

4. Eric loses some red markers. Now there are only 6 red markers left. How many red markers did he lose?

○ 16
○ 9
○ 5
○ 4

5. **Stretch Your Thinking** Make a table that shows the following information about trees in a park. There are twice as many oak trees as elm trees. There are 3 fewer maple trees than oak trees.

     Collect and Graph Data

Homework

Books Read

Benita	
Lin	
Diego	
Marcus	

0 1 2 3 4 5 6 7 8 9 10

Use the bar graph to solve the problems.

1. Benita read 4 history books. The rest were science books. How many science books did she read?

   ☐ _____
   label

2. Marcus read 3 fewer books than Gina. How many books did Gina read?

   ☐ _____
   label

3. Diego read 4 more books than Eva. How many books did Eva read?

   ☐ _____
   label

4. How many more books did Marcus and Diego read than Benita and Lin?

   ☐ _____
   label

5. Ali read 4 more books than Lin and Marcus. How many books did Ali read?

   ☐ _____
   label

Remembering

Subtract.

1.
$$\begin{array}{r} 18 \\ -\ 9 \\ \hline \end{array}$$
$$\begin{array}{r} 14 \\ -\ 8 \\ \hline \end{array}$$
$$\begin{array}{r} 10 \\ -\ 3 \\ \hline \end{array}$$
$$\begin{array}{r} 15 \\ -\ 9 \\ \hline \end{array}$$
$$\begin{array}{r} 16 \\ -\ 7 \\ \hline \end{array}$$
$$\begin{array}{r} 11 \\ -\ 5 \\ \hline \end{array}$$

2. Zoe makes a bracelet with 4 square beads,
1 oval bead, and 9 heart beads. Make a table
to show this.

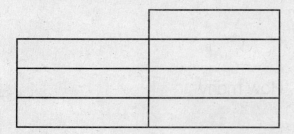

3. Use the information in the table to make a picture
graph. Use a circle for each bead.

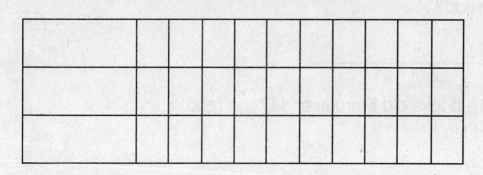

4. **Stretch Your Thinking** Tell something the
graph shows.

Name

Homework

Ms. Morgan asked the children in her class which
of these pets they liked best.

Which Is Your Favorite Pet?

Dog	○ ○ ○ ○ ○ ○ ○ ○ ○
Cat	○ ○ ○ ○ ○ ○
Bird	○ ○ ○ ○
Fish	○ ○ ○ ○ ○

1. Use the information in the table to make a bar graph.

Title:_____

_____

_____

_____

_____

2. Think about your favorite pet. How would the graph change
if you added your own answer to the question?

_____

_____

Name _____

Remembering

Write how to count the money.

1.

25¢   35¢   ___   ___   ___   ___   ___

Use the bar graph to solve the problems.

Crayons in Box

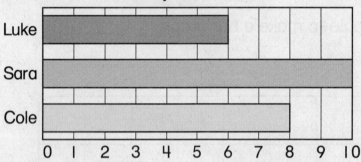

2. Five of Sara's crayons are new. The rest are old.
   How many crayons are old?

   ☐ _____

3. Alexa has 3 more crayons than Luke. How many
   crayons does Alexa have?

   ☐ _____

4. **Stretch Your Thinking** Look at the bar graph.
   Explain what could change so that everyone has
   the same number of crayons.

   _____

   _____

Focus on Mathematical Practices

Homework

Count the hundreds, tens, and ones.
Write the totals.

1. ☐ ||||| |||| ⦾⦾⦾⦾⦾ ⦾⦾⦾

_____   _____   _____   Total _____
Hundreds   Tens   Ones

---

2. ☐☐☐☐ ||||| ⦾⦾⦾⦾⦾ ⦾⦾⦾⦾

_____   _____   _____   Total _____
Hundreds   Tens   Ones

Draw to show the numbers. Use boxes, sticks, and circles.

3. ___2___   ___4___   ___3___   4. ___4___   ___6___   ___8___
   Hundreds   Tens   Ones   Hundreds   Tens   Ones

---

5. ___3___   ___8___   ___2___   6. ___1___   ___7___   ___7___
   Hundreds   Tens   Ones   Hundreds   Tens   Ones

Remembering

Add.

1. 43
  + 28

2. 65
  + 17

3. 35
  + 28

4. 52
  + 38

5. 47
  + 29

Write <, >, or =.

6. 153 ◯ 181

7. 113 ◯ 131

8. 56 ◯ 104

9. 59 ◯ 59

10. 84 ◯ 48

11. 151 ◯ 139

12. Write how to count the money.

25¢ _____ _____ _____ _____ _____

13. **Stretch Your Thinking** You have base ten blocks for 2 hundreds, 2 tens, and 2 ones. Write all of the different 3-digit numbers you could show.

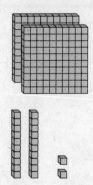

_____

_____

Homework

Write the hundreds, tens, and ones.

1. $675 =$ _600_ + _70_ + _5_
   H T O

2. $519 =$ _____ + _____ + _____

3. $831 =$ _____ + _____ + _____

4. $487 =$ _____ + _____ + _____

5. $222 =$ _____ + _____ + _____

6. $765 =$ _____ + _____ + _____

Write the number.

7. $300 + 40 + 6 =$ _346_
   H T O

8. $100 + 60$ $=$ _____

9. $700 +$ $4 =$ _____

10. $200 + 50 + 3 =$ _____

11. $400 + 70 + 1 =$ _____

12. $800 + 80 + 8 =$ _____

Write the number that makes the equation true.

13. _____ $= 30 + 5 + 400$

14. $2 + 80 + 600 =$ _____

15. _____ $= 60 + 800$

16. $900 + 7 + 40 =$ _____

17. _____ $= 300 + 4 + 50$

18. $1 + 500$ $=$ _____

19. $729 = 20 + 9 +$ _____

20. _____ $+ 6 + 200 = 296$

Remembering

Add in any order. Write the total.

1. $8 + 1 + 4 =$ ☐

2. $6 + 9 + 5 =$ ☐

3. $7 + 4 + 3 =$ ☐

4. $8 + 3 + 2 =$ ☐

Draw a Math Mountain to solve the word problem.
Show how you add or subtract.

Show your work.

5. There are 23 girls and 49 boys
standing in line. How many
children are standing in line?

☐ _____
label

6. Count the hundreds, tens, and ones.
Write the total.

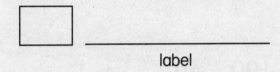

____ ____   ____ ____   ____ ____   Total _____

Hundreds   Tens   Ones

7. Stretch Your Thinking Write an addition equation.
The equation must have a 1-, a 2-, and a 3-digit
addend and use all of these digits.

6 6 2 2 8 8 0 0 0

_____

_____

Homework

Write <, >, or =.

1. 285 ◯ 385

2. 452 ◯ 425

3. 961 ◯ 691

4. 199 ◯ 205

5. 754 ◯ 861

6. 738 ◯ 694

7. 367 ◯ 67

8. 274 ◯ 274

9. 158 ◯ 159

10. 106 ◯ 99

11. 222 ◯ 333

12. 73 ◯ 511

13. 604 ◯ 604

14. 138 ◯ 136

15. 288 ◯ 386

16. 207 ◯ 197

17. 648 ◯ 734

18. 549 ◯ 559

19. 762 ◯ 643

20. 709 ◯ 810

21. 691 ◯ 961

22. 802 ◯ 802

Remembering

Be the helper. Is the answer OK? Write *yes* or *no*.
If *no*, fix the mistakes and write the correct answer.

1.   28   OK?   2.   58   OK?   3.   45   OK?
    + 34   ☐   + 17   ☐   + 26   ☐
    ——   ——   ——
      62   515   61

Add up to solve the word problem.   **Show your work.**

4. Allison has 67 beads. She uses some beads to
   make a necklace. Now she has 39 beads. How
   many beads did Allison use for her necklace?

   ☐ _____
        label

Write the number.

5. 400 + 10 + 5 = _____   6. 800 + 7 = _____

7. **Stretch Your Thinking** Use the digits to write pairs of 3-digit numbers.
   Write <, >, or = to compare the pairs of numbers you write.

                6   1   3   7   2   0

   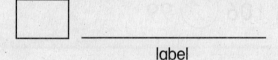

Name _____

Homework

Count by ones. Write the numbers.

1. 396 397 _398_ _399_ _400_ _401_ _402_ _403_ 404

2. 695 696 ____ ____ ____ ____ ____ ____ 703

3. 498 499 ____ ____ ____ ____ ____ ____ 506

4. 894 ____ ____ ____ ____ ____ ____ ____ 902

5. 796 ____ ____ ____ ____ ____ ____ ____ 804

Count by tens. Write the numbers.

6. 830 840 _850_ _860_ _870_ _880_ _890_ _900_ 910

7. 470 480 ____ ____ ____ ____ ____ ____ 550

8. 740 ____ ____ ____ ____ ____ ____ ____ 820

9. 380 ____ ____ ____ ____ ____ ____ ____ 460

10. 560 ____ ____ ____ ____ ____ ____ ____ 640

Write the number name.

11. 597 _____

12. 640 _____

Remembering

Find the total or partner.

1.   4   9   7   13   16   18
    + 8   + 6   + 5   − 7   − 9   − 9
    ───   ───   ───   ───   ───   ───

Solve the word problem.   **Show your work.**

2. Cameron reads 57 pages on Monday and
   85 pages on Tuesday. How many pages
   does he read in all?

   ┌──────────┐   _____
   │   │
   └──────────┘
        label

Write <. >, or =.

3. 675 ◯ 657   4. 198 ◯ 201

5. 86 ◯ 124   6. 36 ◯ 36

7. **Stretch Your Thinking** Natalie practices the piano
   every day. On Monday she practiced for 10 minutes.
   If she practices every day for 10 minutes, on which
   day of the week will she have practiced for
   90 minutes? Explain.

   _____

   _____

   _____

© Houghton Mifflin Harcourt Publishing Company

Homework

Solve each word problem.

1. Maria blows up some balloons for a party. She divides them into 4 groups of one hundred and 7 groups of ten. There are 6 balloons left over. How many balloons does Maria blow up for the party?

_____
label

2. Roger has 5 erasers. He buys 6 packages of one hundred and 2 packages of ten. How many erasers does Roger have altogether?

_____
label

3. Add.

$400 + 200 =$ _____

$40 + 50 =$ _____

$8 + 460 =$ _____

$30 + 10 =$ _____

$380 + 10 =$ _____

$440 + 7 =$ _____

$84 + 10 =$ _____

$200 + 9 =$ _____

$60 + 40 =$ _____

$900 + 80 =$ _____

$16 + 700 =$ _____

$70 + 7 =$ _____

$53 + 500 =$ _____

$60 + 4 =$ _____

$800 + 200 =$ _____

Remembering

Look for shapes around you.

1. List or draw objects that show rectangles.

Solve the word problem. Draw a
proof drawing if you need to.

Show your work.

2. There are 200 people with tickets for the
Fall Festival. A worker collects tickets
from 62 of the people. How many tickets
are still left to collect?

_____
label

Count by tens. Write the numbers.

3. 650 660 _____ _____ _____ _____ _____ _____ 730

4. Stretch Your Thinking Brian has some boxes of
paper clips. Some boxes hold 10 clips and some
boxes hold 100. He has some paper clips left over.
He has three more boxes with 100 paper clips than
he has boxes with 10 paper clips. He has two fewer
paper clips left over than he has numbers of boxes
with 100 paper clips. What number of paper clips
could he have?

_____

Add Ones, Tens, and Hundreds

Homework

Solve each word problem.

1. Martin sells 58 tickets to the roller coaster ride. He sells 267 tickets to the boat ride. How many tickets does Martin sell altogether?

2. Justine jumps 485 times on a pogo stick. Then she jumps 329 times when she tries again. How many times does she jump altogether?

_____
label

_____
label

Add.

3. $18 + 549 =$ ☐

4. $190 + 89 =$ ☐

5. $76 + 570 =$ ☐

6. $75 + 656 =$ ☐

7. $348 + 162 =$ ☐

8. $407 + 394 =$ ☐

Name _____

Remembering

Add. Use any method.

1. 53
  + 39
  ____

2. 45
  + 86
  ____

3. 75
  + 68
  ____

Label the shapes using the words in the box.

| cube   quadrilateral   pentagon   hexagon |

4.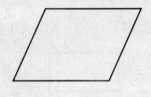

_____

5.

_____

Add.

6. 300 + 70 = _____   20 + 40 = _____   8 + 650 = _____

---

7. **Stretch Your Thinking** Add a 3-digit number
   and a 2-digit number. Use the digits 5, 6, 7,
   and 8 to write the addition exercise. You can
   use a digit more than once. Find the sum.

   _____

3-Digit Addition

Homework

Add. Use any method.

1. 459
   + 267

Make a new ten? _____
Make a new hundred? _____
Make a new thousand? _____

2. 187 + 374 = _____

Make a new ten? _____
Make a new hundred? _____
Make a new thousand? _____

3. 678
   + 15

Make a new ten? _____
Make a new hundred? _____
Make a new thousand? _____

4. 635 + 92 = _____

Make a new ten? _____
Make a new hundred? _____
Make a new thousand? _____

5. 390
   + 610

Make a new ten? _____
Make a new hundred? _____
Make a new thousand? _____

6. 64 + 936 = _____

Make a new ten? _____
Make a new hundred? _____
Make a new thousand? _____

© Houghton Mifflin Harcourt Publishing Company

Remembering

Measure each vertical line segment below by
marking and counting 1-cm lengths.

1.   **2.**   **3.**

[ ] cm   [ ] cm   [ ] cm

Solve the word problem.

4. A man sells 275 circus tickets on Monday
morning and 369 circus tickets on Monday
afternoon. How many tickets does he
sell on Monday?

[ ] _____
         label

---

5. Stretch Your Thinking Write an addition exercise
with a sum of 1,000. Use two 3-digit addends. Choose
addends so that you will need to make a new ten,
a new hundred, and a new thousand when you add.

_____

_____

Discuss 3-Digit Addition

Homework

Solve each word problem.   **Show your work.**

1. Angie has 648 stickers. 254 of the stickers
   are cat stickers. The rest are dog stickers.
   How many dog stickers does Angie have?

   [   ] _____
                    label

2. Billy has 315 coins. 209 of the coins are
   silver in color. How many coins are not
   silver in color?

   [   ] _____
                    label

3. Noah is going to plant 752 seeds. Some
   of the seeds are flower seeds. 547 of the
   seeds are vegetable seeds. How many
   flower seeds will Noah plant?

   [   ] _____
                    label

4. Heather's dad is reading a book that is 564
   pages long. So far he has read 286 pages.
   How many pages does he have left to read?

   [   ] _____
                    label

Name _____

Remembering

Make a ten to find the total.

1. $7 + 6 =$ ☐

2. $8 + 7 =$ ☐

3. $8 + 9 =$ ☐

Write the time in two different ways.

4.

_____ o'clock

5.

_____ o'clock

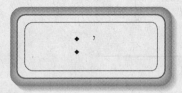

6.

_____ o'clock

Add. Use any method.

7. $\begin{array}{r} 357 \\ + 585 \\ \hline \end{array}$

Make a new ten? _____

Make a new hundred? _____

Make a new thousand? _____

8. $249 + 751 =$ _____

Make a new ten? _____

Make a new hundred? _____

Make a new thousand? _____

9. Stretch Your Thinking Explain how to solve for an unknown addend.

_____

_____

Word Problems: Unknown Addends

Name _____

Homework

Solve the word problems. Use your favorite
method. Make a proof drawing.

1. Ricardo likes olives. He has
100 olives. He eats 43 of them.
How many olives does he have
left?

[   ] _____
            label

2. Dawn has 1,000 pennies in her
penny jar. She gives some to her
sister. Now she has 432 left. How
many pennies does Dawn give to
her sister?

[   ] _____
            label

3. Tory sells hockey sticks to teams
in her city. She has 500 and sells
353. How many hockey sticks
does she have left to sell?

[   ] _____
            label

4. Randy collects magnets. Over
two years he collects 400 magnets.
He collects 125 magnets the first
year. How many does he collect
the second year?

[   ] _____
            label

Remembering

Add.

1. $5 + 6 =$ _____ $7 + 9 =$ _____ $100 + 35 =$ _____

    $50 + 60 =$ _____ $70 + 90 =$ _____ $10 + 35 =$ _____

                                                  $1 + 35 =$ _____

Draw hands on each clock to show the time.

2.    3.    4.    5.

| 4:10 | 1:30 |  7:15 | 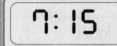 10:45 |

Solve the word problem.

6. The school has 537 children. 359 of the children had lunch. How many children still need to have lunch?

   [ ] _____
           label

7. **Stretch Your Thinking** How is subtracting from a 3-digit number different from subtracting from a 2-digit number?

   _____

   _____

   _____

Homework

Decide if you need to ungroup. If you need to ungroup, draw a magnifying glass around the top number. Then find the answer.

1.
```
  7 3 0
- 4 9 9
```

Ungroup to get 10 ones? _____

Ungroup to get 10 tens? _____

2.
```
  9 5 0
- 6 3 9
```

Ungroup to get 10 ones? _____

Ungroup to get 10 tens? _____

3.
```
  3 0 0
- 1 6 7
```

Ungroup to get 10 ones? _____

Ungroup to get 10 tens? _____

4.
```
  4 0 4
- 1 8 8
```

Ungroup to get 10 ones? _____

Ungroup to get 10 tens? _____

6. 502 − 149 = _____

5.
```
  4 2 0
- 1 8 3
```

Ungroup to get 10 ones? _____

Ungroup to get 10 tens? _____

Ungroup to get 10 ones? _____

Ungroup to get 10 tens? _____

Subtract from Numbers with Zeros

Name _____

Remembering

Use the picture graph to answer the questions.

Crayons

Paige	✏	✏	✏	✏	✏	✏	✏	✏	✏
Tawana	✏	✏							
Colin	✏	✏	✏	✏	✏				

1. Who has the most crayons? _____

2. Who has the fewest crayons? _____

3. How many crayons do they all have together?

   ▢ _____
   label

Solve the word problem. Use your favorite method.
Make a proof drawing.

4. There are 500 craft sticks in the box.
   The art class uses 386 of the craft sticks.
   How many craft sticks are left?

   ▢ _____
   label

5. **Stretch Your Thinking** When you are subtracting
   from a 3-digit number, how do you know if you will
   need to ungroup?

   _____

   _____

Subtract from Numbers with Zeros

Name _____

Homework

Decide if you need to ungroup. If you need to ungroup,
draw a magnifying glass around the top number.
Then find the answer.

1.
$$
\begin{array}{r}
5\ 3\ 1 \\
-\ 4\ 3\ 4 \\
\hline
\end{array}
$$

Ungroup to get 10 ones? _____

Ungroup to get 10 tens? _____

2.
$$
\begin{array}{r}
5\ 7\ 9 \\
-\ 2\ 9\ 6 \\
\hline
\end{array}
$$

Ungroup to get 10 ones? _____

Ungroup to get 10 tens? _____

3.
$$
\begin{array}{r}
3\ 9\ 1 \\
-\ 2\ 6\ 5 \\
\hline
\end{array}
$$

Ungroup to get 10 ones? _____

Ungroup to get 10 tens? _____

4. $238 - 177 =$ _____

Ungroup to get 10 ones? _____

Ungroup to get 10 tens? _____

5. Latoya's class picks 572 apples on a field trip. They bring 386 apples home with them. How many apples do they leave?

[ ] _____
label

6. Elena had 735 stickers. She gives 427 stickers to her brother. How many stickers does she have left?

[ ] _____
label

Remembering

Subtract.

1.	61	2.	85	3.	93	4.	52	5.	91
	− 25		− 34		− 24		− 23		− 54

Read the picture graph.
Write the number. Ring *more* or *fewer*.

Number of Marbles

Ling	🔵 🔵 🔵 🔵 🔵
Sean	🔵 🔵 🔵 🔵 🔵 🔵 🔵 🔵 🔵 🔵 🔵
Maya	🔵 🔵 🔵 🔵 🔵 🔵 🔵

6. Sean has ☐ *more fewer* marbles than Ling.

7. Maya needs ☐ *more fewer* marbles to have as many marbles as Sean.

Decide if you need to ungroup. If you need to ungroup, draw a magnifying glass around the top number. Then find the answer.

8. 863
     − 245

Ungroup to get 10 ones? _____

Ungroup to get 10 tens? _____

9. Stretch Your Thinking Write and solve a subtraction exercise in which you need to ungroup two times.

Subtract from Any 3-Digit Number

Homework

Decide if you need to ungroup. If you need to ungroup,
draw a magnifying glass around the top number. Then
find the answer.

1.   6 3 0
    − 3 1 8
    _____

Ungroup to get 10 ones? _____

Ungroup to get 10 tens? _____

2.   9 3 1
    − 8 4 5
    _____

Ungroup to get 10 ones? _____

Ungroup to get 10 tens? _____

3.   4 0 7
    − 2 7 4
    _____

Ungroup to get 10 ones? _____

Ungroup to get 10 tens? _____

4.   4 9 8
    − 2 7 6
    _____

Ungroup to get 10 ones? _____

Ungroup to get 10 tens? _____

5. Jamal has 590 craft sticks. He
uses 413 craft sticks to make a
building. How many craft sticks
does he have left?

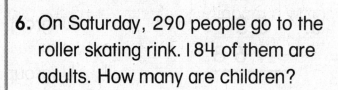

_____
label

6. On Saturday, 290 people go to the
roller skating rink. 184 of them are
adults. How many are children?

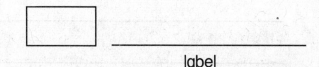

_____
label

Remembering

Under each picture, write the total amount of
money so far. Then write the total using $.

1. 100¢   25¢   1¢   1¢

_____   _____   _____   _____ $ ___.___ ___
                                                    total

Make a drawing. Write an equation. Solve.

2. Jiao has some beads. Then she buys
   35 more beads. Now she has 73 beads.
   How many beads did Jiao start with?

   ☐ _____
            label

Decide if you need to ungroup. If you need
to ungroup, draw a magnifying glass around
the top number. Then find the answer.

3.   5 3 7   Ungroup to get 10 ones? _____
   − 1 6 8
   _____   Ungroup to get 10 tens? _____

4. **Stretch Your Thinking** What 3-digit number
   would need no ungrouping to subtract from? Explain.

   _____

   _____

Practice Ungrouping

Homework

Decide if you need to add or subtract. Use the
opposite operation to check your answer.

1.　　184
　　 +433

2.　　552
　　 −399

3.　　328
　　 −119

4.　　288
　　 +294

5. 967 − 548 = _____

6. 474 − 355 = _____

Name _____

Remembering

Use the bar graph to complete the sentences.

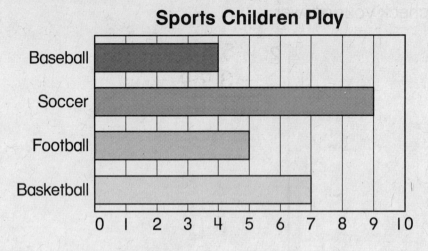

Sports Children Play

1. Four fewer children play _____ than soccer.

2. Eleven children play _____ or _____.

Decide if you need to ungroup. If you need to ungroup, draw a magnifying glass around the top number. Then find the answer.

3.   427
   − 159
   ‾‾‾‾‾

Ungroup to get 10 ones? _____

Ungroup to get 10 tens? _____

4. **Stretch Your Thinking** Explain why you can check subtraction by adding.

_____

_____

_____

© Houghton Mifflin Harcourt Publishing Company

Homework

Solve each word problem.

1. Mario buys 98 plastic cups. He gives 29 to the art teacher. How many cups does he have left?

□ _____
     label

2. Joel collects baseball cards. He has 568 cards. Then he buys 329 more at a yard sale. How many cards does he have now?

□ _____
     label

3. A bird collects 392 sticks to build a nest. Then the bird collects 165 more. How many sticks does the bird collect?

□ _____
     label

4. There are 765 books in the school library. 259 are paperback, and the rest are hardcover. How many hardcover books are there in the school library?

□ _____
     label

Name _____

Remembering

Make a drawing. Write an equation. Solve the problem.

1. There are some children in the class.
8 are girls and 9 are boys. How many
children are in the class?

☐ _____
                    label

Estimate and then measure each side.
Then find the distance around the triangle.

2.

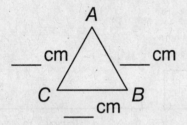

a. Complete the table.

Side	Estimate	Measure
AB		
BC		
CA		

b. Find the distance around the triangle.

_____ cm + _____ cm + _____ cm = _____ cm

Decide if you need to add or subtract. Use the
opposite operation to check your answer.

3.   6 8 3
       − 1 4 5

4.   2 5 7
       + 3 6 9

5. Stretch Your Thinking Write and solve a subtraction
word problem with an answer greater than 500 pennies.

_____

_____

_____

Mixed Addition and Subtraction Word Problems

Homework

The table shows the number of children who take part in different after school activities.

Use the table to solve the word problems.

Show your work.

After School Activities	
Activity	**Number of Children**
Art Club	378
Music Lessons	205
Sports	204
Dance Class	105
Science Club	217

1. One hundred seventeen girls take music lessons after school. How many boys take music lessons?

   ☐ _____

   label

2. How many fewer children signed up for music and dance than signed up for the art club?

   ☐ _____

   label

3. Write a word problem using data from the table. Solve the problem.

   _____

   _____

   _____

Remembering

Estimate and then measure each side.
Then find the distance around the rectangle.

1.

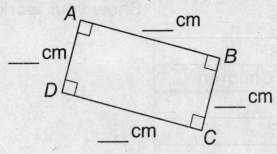

a. Complete the table.

Side	Estimate	Measure
AB		
BC		
CD		
DA		

b. Find the distance around the rectangle.

_____ cm + _____ cm + _____ cm + _____ cm = _____ cm

Solve the word problem.

2. The store has 374 CDs. A box with
   258 CDs arrives at the store. How
   many CDs does the store have now?

   [ ] _____
           label

---

3. **Stretch Your Thinking** Fill in the digits to
   complete the addition exercise.

```
   1  □  4
+  □  6  □
_____
   4  5  1
```

Homework

Write how many in each row and in each column.
Then write two equations for each array.

I.

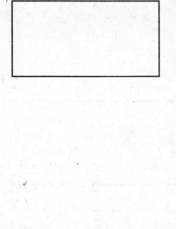 _____
_____
_____
_____
_____

_____ _____ _____ _____

_____

_____

2.

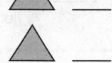 _____

_____

_____

_____

_____

Measure in centimeters. Draw rows and columns.
Write the number of small squares.

3.

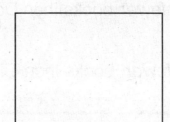

4.

5.

_____ squares

_____ squares

_____ squares

Remembering

Make a matching drawing or draw comparison bars.
Solve the problem.

1. Al has 8 grapes. Erin has 6 more grapes than
   Al. How many grapes does Erin have?

   ☐ _____

          label

Read the picture graph.
Write the number. Ring *more* or *fewer.*

Number of Books

David	☐ ☐ ☐
Tiffany	☐ ☐ ☐ ☐ ☐ ☐ ☐ ☐ ☐ ☐
Pedro	☐ ☐ ☐ ☐ ☐ ☐

2. Tiffany has ☐ *more fewer* books than David.

3. Pedro has ☐ *more fewer* books than Tiffany.

Count by tens. Write the numbers.

4. 650 _____ _____ _____ _____ _____ _____ 730

5. **Stretch Your Thinking** Draw three different
   arrays that show 12.

    Arrays, Partitioned Rectangles, and Equal Shares

Homework

I. Make 2 halves. Show different ways.
Shade half of each rectangle.

 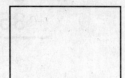  

2. Make 3 thirds. Show different ways.
Shade a third of each rectangle.

3. Make 4 fourths. Show different ways.
Shade a fourth of each rectangle.

4. Make 2 halves.
Shade half of
the circle.

5. Make 3 thirds.
Shade a third of
the circle.

6. Make 4 fourths.
Shade a fourth of
the circle.

Remembering

Add.

1. 73
   + 19
   ___

2. 53
   + 46
   ___

3. 68
   + 23
   ___

4. 27
   + 35
   ___

5. 46
   + 39
   ___

Write how many in each row and in each column.
Then write two equations for each array.

6.

_____ circles in an array with lines for each row

___
___
___
___
___

___   ___   ___

_____

_____

7.

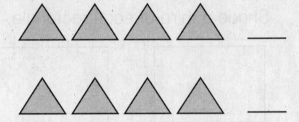

___

___

___

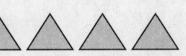

_____

_____

8. **Stretch Your Thinking** Draw a rectangle.
   Show 4 fourths that are all the same-size
   triangles, but not all the same shape.

Find Equal Shares

Homework

Solve.   **Show your work.**

1. Becky's garden is 21 meters wide.
   Jerry's garden is 17 meters wide.
   How much wider is Becky's garden
   than Jerry's garden?

   ☐ _____
         unit

2. Hannah's painting is 39 inches long.
   She adds 12 inches to it. How long
   is the painting now?

   ☐ _____
         unit

Use the number line diagram to add or subtract.

3. Loop 28 and 56. Loop the difference D.

   How long is it? _____

   ←|┼┼┼┼|┼┼┼┼|┼┼┼┼|┼┼┼┼|┼┼┼┼|┼┼┼┼|┼┼┼┼|┼┼┼┼|┼┼┼┼|┼┼┼┼|┼┼┼┼|┼┼┼┼|┼┼┼┼|┼┼┼┼|┼┼┼┼|┼┼┼┼|┼┼┼┼|┼┼┼┼|┼┼┼┼|┼┼┼┼|→

   0   5   10   15   20   25   30   35   40   45   50   55   60   65   70   75   80   85   90   95 100

4. Loop 48. Add 15 to it. Loop the total T.

   How long is it? _____

   ←|┼┼┼┼|┼┼┼┼|┼┼┼┼|┼┼┼┼|┼┼┼┼|┼┼┼┼|┼┼┼┼|┼┼┼┼|┼┼┼┼|┼┼┼┼|┼┼┼┼|┼┼┼┼|┼┼┼┼|┼┼┼┼|┼┼┼┼|┼┼┼┼|┼┼┼┼|┼┼┼┼|┼┼┼┼|┼┼┼┼|→

   0   5   10   15   20   25   30   35   40   45   50   55   60   65   70   75   80   85   90   95 100

Remembering

Add.

1. $14 + 46 + 62 + 39 =$ [ ]

2. Count the hundreds, tens, and ones.

   Write the total.

   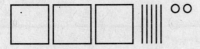

   _____   _____   _____   Total _____
   Hundreds   Tens   Ones

3. Make 2 halves.

4. Make 3 thirds.

5. Make 4 fourths.

6. **Stretch Your Thinking** Write a subtraction word problem that has the answer *6 feet*.

   _____

   _____

   _____

   _____

Problems About Length and Number Line Diagrams

Homework

Solve.   **Show your work.**

1. Here is the path Fluffy took on her walk today. How many meters did she walk?

   ☐ _____
        unit

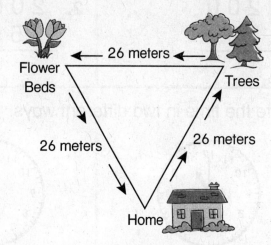

2. Colin wants to decorate a picture frame with gold ribbon. How long should the ribbon be if he wants to put ribbon around the whole frame?

   ☐ _____
        unit

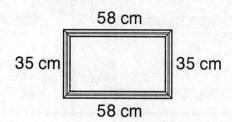

3. Here is a top view drawing of the new sandbox for the park. Each side is 16 feet long. A border runs along the edge. How long is the border?

   ☐ _____
        unit

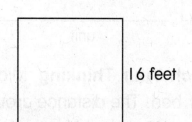

Name _____

Remembering

Subtract.

1. $\begin{array}{r} 2\,0\,0 \\ -\ \ 4\,1 \\ \hline \end{array}$	2. $\begin{array}{r} 2\,0\,0 \\ -\ \ 5\,5 \\ \hline \end{array}$	3. $\begin{array}{r} 2\,0\,0 \\ -\ \ 8\,7 \\ \hline \end{array}$

Write the time in two different ways.

4. 	5. 	6. 
_____ o'clock	_____ o'clock	_____ o'clock
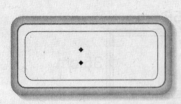	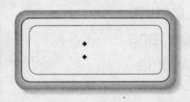	

Solve.   **Show your work.**

7. Jen's paper is 30 cm long. She cuts
   12 cm from the bottom of the paper.
   How long is her paper now?

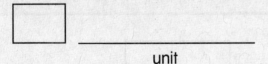

   unit

8. **Stretch Your Thinking** Michael has a triangle-shaped
   flower bed. The distance around the flower bed is
   58 feet. What could be the length of each side?

_____

_____

Add Three and Four Lengths

Homework

Represent each equation on the number line diagram.
Then find the difference or the total.

1. $56 + \boxed{} = 94$

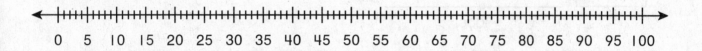

2. $34 + 47 = \boxed{}$

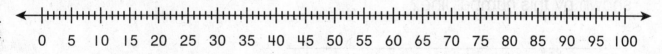

3. $\boxed{} + 31 = 69$

4. $42 + 29 = \boxed{}$

Name _____

Remembering

Solve. Rewrite the 100 or make a drawing.   **Show your work.**
Add to check your answer.

1. Brian sees 100 cars in the parking lot.
   36 of the cars leave. How many cars
   are still in the parking lot?

   ```
   ┌─────────┐
   │         │   _____
   └─────────┘        label
   ```

Solve.

2. Mr. Kensey is putting a fence around
   his garden. How much fencing will he
   need if he wants to put a fence around
   the whole garden?

   ```
   ┌─────────┐
   │         │   _____
   └─────────┘        unit
   ```

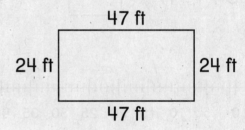

---

3. **Stretch Your Thinking** What equation is
   shown by this number line?

   _____

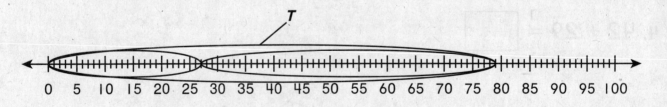

More Length Word Problems

Name _____

Homework

1. Show 2 halves.

2. Show 3 thirds.

3. Show 4 fourths.

Roberto, Niko, and Maya each buy a pizza.
All their pizzas are the same size.

- Roberto cuts his pizza into 2 equal parts.

- Niko cuts his pizza into 3 equal parts.

- Maya cuts her pizza into 4 equal parts.

4. Roberto eats 2 halves and Maya eats 4 fourths.
Do they eat the same amount? Explain.

_____

_____

_____

5. Is half of Roberto's pizza greater than, less than,
or equal to a third of Maya's pizza? Explain.

_____

_____

_____

Remembering

Subtract.

1. 73
    − 45

2. 91
    − 37

3. 68
    − 34

4. 83
    − 18

5. 50
    − 37

Estimate and then measure each side.
Then find the distance around the triangle.

6.

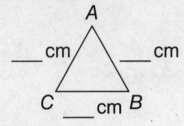

a. Complete the table.

Side	Estimate	Measure
AB		
BC		
CA		

b. Find the distance around the triangle.

_____ cm + _____ cm + _____ cm = _____ cm

Show the equation on the number line diagram.
Then find the difference or the total.

7. 35 + ☐ = 78

0 5 10 15 20 25 30 35 40 45 50 55 60 65 70 75 80 85 90 95 100

8. Stretch Your Thinking Dennis and Tami each make a
pizza. Both pizzas are the same size and shape. Dennis
eats 4 pieces. Tami eats 2 pieces. Could they each have
eaten the same amount? Explain.

_____

_____